Topic 1

The measurement of economic performance

The objectives of government economic policy

The government has a number of goals — objectives — that it wishes to achieve for the economy. These include achieving economic growth, minimising unemployment, achieving stable prices, balancing the budget on the government's finances as well as achieving balance on foreign trade.

Sometimes, there will be a policy conflict which means achieving one objective moves us further away from achieving other objectives. However, some would argue that these policy conflicts — if they exist at all — only exist in the short run; in the long run it might be possible to achieve (or move closer to achieving) all objectives simultaneously.

---

1 Define the term 'current account'. (AO1) **3 marks**

....

....

....

2 Which of the following would feature in the current account of the balance of payments? (AO1) **2 marks**

- **Exports of goods**
- **Taxation of imports**
- **Profits earned on overseas investments**
- **Investment expenditure**

....

....

3 Based on the following data, calculate the rate of economic growth between year 1 and year 2. (AO1, AO2) **4 marks**

	GDP (£ million)
Year 1	1,992,000
Year 2	2,061,720

....

....

....

....

④ Explain why falling economic growth is different from negative economic growth. (AO1, AO2)

4 marks

....

....

....

....

⑤ The following table relates to the output of an economy and the number of people in employment.

	Output (units)	Number in employment
Year 1	145,600	2,000
Year 2	148,400	2,120

a Calculate the productivity per worker for both years. (AO1, AO2)

2 marks

....

....

b Calculate the percentage change in productivity per worker over the time period. (AO2)

2 marks

....

....

Macroeconomic indicators and index numbers

Economic objectives are measured through a number of official indicators, such as real gross domestic product (GDP), real GDP per capita, the inflation rate, the unemployment rate, the budget balance as well as the balance on the current account of the balance of payments.

Macroeconomic indicators are usually expressed in numerical values or rates. Index numbers are a useful way of presenting data.

⑥ Distinguish between the level of unemployment and the unemployment rate. (AO1, AO2)

3 marks

....

....

....

⑦ The table below shows details for a weighted price index which contains only three products, X, Y and Z.

Product	Year 1 price ($)	Year 2 price ($)	Weight
X	8	6	1
Y	16	20	2
Z	20	24	4

If year 1 is the base year, what is the value of the weighted index in year 2? (AO1, AO2)

5 marks

8 The following data relate to a small economy.

Year	Nominal GDP (£m)	Price level
2015	185,600	112
2016	196,560	117

a Calculate the level of real GDP in 2016. (AO1, AO2)

4 marks

b Calculate the inflation rate for the year 2016. (AO1, AO2)

4 marks

c Calculate the level of economic growth in real terms between 2015 and 2016. (AO1, AO2)

4 marks

Uses of national income data

Gross domestic product (GDP) represents the national income for the whole economy. It is often used as a benchmark to represent the standard of living enjoyed within the economy. However, although this approach has its uses, it is not without its limitations. When using GDP to compare living standards between countries, particular care has to be taken to use an appropriate exchange rate. The concept of purchasing power parity (PPP) is useful here in making comparisons more meaningful.

9 State three adjustments that could be made to GDP to make it a more accurate reflection of living standards. (AO1)

3 marks

10 Explain how the actual exchange rate and the purchasing power parity exchange rate differ. (AO1, AO2, AO3) `5 marks`

....

....

....

....

11 UK GDP per capita and French GDP per capita are both close to $40,000 per person, which suggests very similar standards of living in each country. Analyse three reasons why GDP per capita may not reflect living standards that closely. (AO1, AO2, AO3) `9 marks`

....

....

....

....

....

....

....

....

....

....

....

....

8

Exam-style questions: multiple choice

Circle the letter of the answer that you think is correct.

12 The following table shows the prices of two goods (X and Y) over a 4-year period. The base year is year 2.

	Good X	Good Y
Year 1	75	80
Year 2	100	100
Year 3	120	125
Year 4	130	130

Based on these data, which of the following statements can be said to be true? `1 mark`

A Good Y started off the period at a higher price than good X.

B The price of good X rose by a larger percentage over the whole period covered.

C Good Y had the biggest year-on-year price rise measured as a percentage increase.

D In real terms, the price of good Y rose by the least.

⑬ Which of the following is not normally considered to be a useful indicator of economic performance?

A   Balance of payments on current account

B   Index numbers

C   Changes in the consumer price index

D   Levels of claimant count unemployment

⑭ Consider the table below, which includes the output level and employment level for an economy for a 2-year period.

	Output level	Number in employment
Year 1	125	95
Year 2	132	102

From this table, which of the following cannot be concluded?

A   Output levels rose

B   Employment levels rose

C   Productivity increased

D   Productivity decreased

⑮ The table below shows details for a weighted price index which contains only two products, S and T.

Good	Year 1 price ($)	Year 2 price ($)	Weight
S	15	18	1
T	25	18	2

If year 1 is the base year, what is the value of the weighted index in year 2?

A 270	C 100
B 88	D 105

Exam-style questions: data response

⑯ Study Extracts A and B and answer the following questions.

Extract A

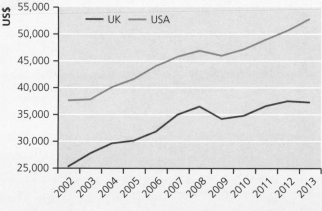

GDP per capita (PPP), 2002–13 (US$)

Extract B

According to the UN, Norway is the best country in the world to live in. The 2015 results once again place Norway as the country with the highest score on the Human Development Index (HDI). It has maintained first place in the HDI rankings now for a number of years, despite only coming in sixth place in terms of income per head (Norway's GDP per capita is $67,000 per person).

Unlike GDP which measures the income of an economy, the HDI tries to give a wider view of the population's wellbeing by including income per person, health and education factors within its calculation. Other countries scoring highly are Australia, Switzerland and Denmark.

The UK comes 14th in the HDI ranking, which is a higher position than if GDP per capita alone is used to rank countries.

Some have argued that GDP per capita is a crude measure of the population's quality of life anyway and that it is a highly flawed statistic. Attempts to come up with a better measurement of quality of life or living standards have not yet been successful, however, and GDP per capita remains the single most used statistic in determining the wellbeing of the population.

a   **If the population of Norway is 5.2 million, then using Extract B, calculate the overall level of GDP for Norway in US$ for 2015.**   2 marks

b   **Explain the term 'purchasing power parity'.**   3 marks

c   **Using the data in Extract A, identify two significant points of comparison between the GDP per capita of the UK and the USA between 2002 and 2013.**   4 marks

d   **Explain two reasons why a government has growth of real GDP as one of its main economic objectives.**   6 marks

e To what extent is HDI a better indicator of the standard of living of a country's population than its GDP per capita?

25 marks

....

....

....

....

....

....

....

....

....

....

....

....

....

....

....

....

....

....

....

....

....

....

....

Exam-style questions: essay

60

Write your answers to the following questions on separate paper and attach them to your book.

17 a Analyse what would be considered 'good' economic performance for the UK economy.

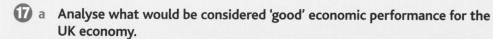

15 marks

b To what extent do you agree that there are inevitably trade-offs when attempting to achieve the government's objectives for the UK economy?

25 marks

9

Topic 2

How the macroeconomy works

National income and the circular flow of income

National income represents the income for the whole economy and this statistic is usually represented by the gross domestic product (GDP) of the economy.

An economic model shows us a simple representation of how the macroeconomy actually works. One such model is the circular flow of income, which shows us how real national income is determined and how national income will rise or fall depending on the actions of households and businesses. In a more complex model of the circular flow, we can see how the government sector and the foreign trade sector influence the level of national income.

1 Explain why real national income provides more useful information than nominal national income. (AO1, AO2) `3 marks`

....

....

....

....

....

2 The following data relate to an economy.

	£ billion
Investment	99
Saving	72
Imports	54
Exports	66
Taxation	88

If this economy is in macroeconomic equilibrium, calculate the level of government expenditure. (AO1, AO2) `4 marks`

....

....

....

....

....

....

Determinants of aggregate demand and the multiplier

Aggregate demand in an economy — the total amount of planned expenditure in an economy — is very important in determining the level of national income, the rate of inflation and the level of unemployment. We can also consider how national income is affected by changes in aggregate demand through the multiplier process and what determines the size of this multiplier.

3 Outline two reasons why the *AD* curve slopes downwards. (AO1, AO2)   4 marks

....

....

....

....

4 In an economy, the following information is available.

- Consumption is £1,450,000 million, of which 25% is spent on imported goods and services.
- Government expenditure is £875,000 million.
- Investment is £475,000.
- There is a trade deficit of £83,600 million.

Based on this information, calculate the level of aggregate demand. (AO1, AO2)   6 marks

....

....

....

....

....

5 For each of the following marginal propensities to consume (*MPCs*), calculate the size of the economic multiplier: (AO1, AO2)   8 marks

a $MPC = 0.9$

b $MPC = 0.6$

c $MPC = 0.75$

d $MPC = \frac{2}{3}$

....

....

....

....

....

....

....

6 For each of the following changes to aggregate demand (*AD*), based on the size of the multiplier, calculate the eventual change to national income. (AO1, AO2)

12 marks

	Change in *AD*	*MPC*	Change to national income
a	Increase by £65m	0.50	
b	Increase by £820m	0.80	
c	Increase by £280m	0.75	
d	Decrease by £115m	0.60	

....

....

....

7 Explain what is meant by the 'reverse multiplier'. (AO1, AO2)   4 marks

....

....

....

....

....

Determinants of aggregate supply

There is a short-run aggregate supply curve for determining macroeconomic equilibrium in the short term, but also a long-run aggregate supply curve which determines the maximum level of output (i.e. full capacity) that can be produced by an economy.

An alternative to short-run and long-run curves is the Keynesian aggregate supply curve.

8 Define the term 'aggregate supply'. (AO1)   3 marks

....

....

....

9 Decide whether the following changes would shift aggregate demand, or short-run aggregate supply. (AO1)

4 marks

5 marks

a   A fall in wage rates ....

b   A rise in business confidence ....

c   A negative wealth effect ....

d   A rise in oil prices ....

e   Advances in technology ....

10 Distinguish between short-run and long-run aggregate supply. (AO1, AO2) `4 marks`

....

....

....

....

11 State which of the following factors would shift short-run aggregate supply and which of them would affect long-run aggregate supply. (AO1) `5 marks`

a An increase in the working population ....

b A temporary rise in oil prices..

c Improvements in training across the economy..

d Higher minimum wage rates..

e Cuts in benefits paid to the unemployed ....

12 Draw a Keynesian aggregate supply curve and analyse why it differs from the *SRAS/LRAS* approach. (AO1, AO2, AO3) `9 marks`

Aggregate demand and aggregate supply analysis

How *AD* and *AS* interact is very important as the resulting equilibrium will also affect other macroeconomic variables, such as the unemployment rate as well as the government's budget balance and the foreign trade balance. They allow us to see how their interaction leads to an equilibrium level of real national income as well as the price level at that level of output. We can see how changes in the behaviour of the different groups in the economy, such as households, will affect the equilibrium position for the economy.

⓭ The following diagram shows a shift in the *LRAS* of an economy.

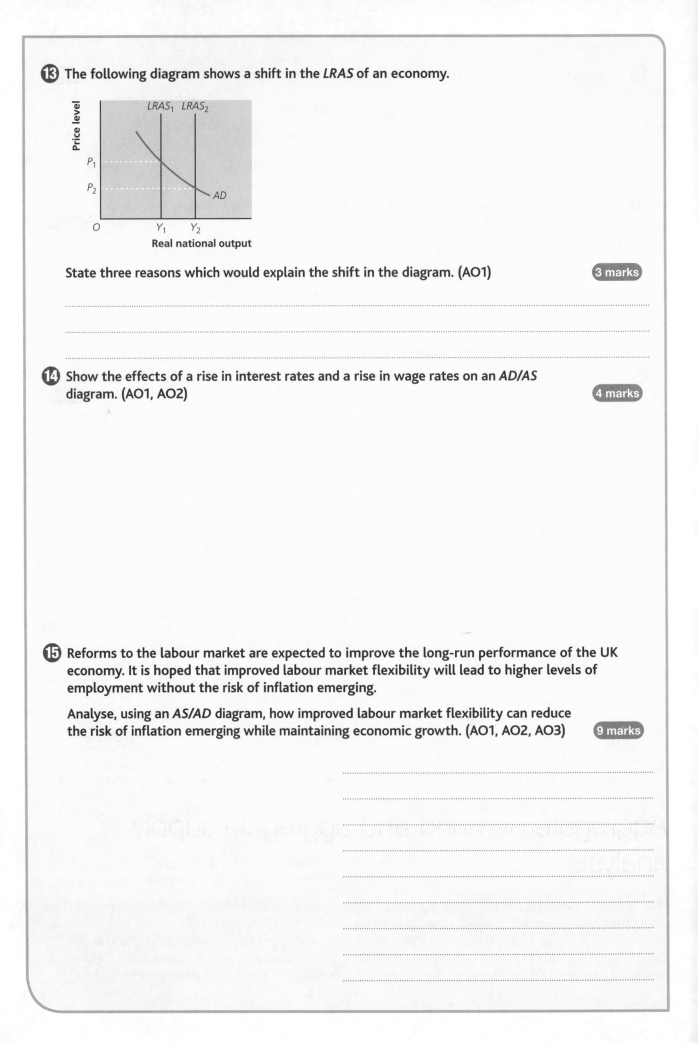

State three reasons which would explain the shift in the diagram. (AO1)

3 marks

....

....

....

⓮ Show the effects of a rise in interest rates and a rise in wage rates on an *AD/AS* diagram. (AO1, AO2)

4 marks

⓯ Reforms to the labour market are expected to improve the long-run performance of the UK economy. It is hoped that improved labour market flexibility will lead to higher levels of employment without the risk of inflation emerging.

Analyse, using an *AS/AD* diagram, how improved labour market flexibility can reduce the risk of inflation emerging while maintaining economic growth. (AO1, AO2, AO3)

9 marks

....

....

....

....

....

....

....

....

16 Show the impact on national output and prices of an increase in government expenditure using an *AD/AS* diagram. Explain why it matters what assumptions are made about the shape of the *AS* curve. (AO1, AO2, AO3)   `9 marks`

....

....

....

....

....

....

....

....

....

....

....

Exam-style questions: multiple choice

Circle the letter of the answer that you think is correct.

17 The diagram below shows a shift from AD_1 to AD_2 in the aggregate demand curve for an economy.

Which of the following would explain the shift in the *AD* curve?   `1 mark`

A   Lower price level

B   Wealth effect of higher house prices

C   Fall in the exchange rate

D   Lower government expenditure

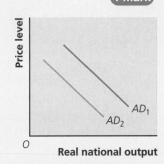

18 An economy has a marginal propensity to consume of 0.6. A rise in government expenditure leads to an eventual rise in national income of £375 million.

What was the size of the original increase in government expenditure?   `1 mark`

A   £150 million

B   £75 million

C   £225 million

D   £62.5 million

19 These diagrams show *AD* and *SRAS* curves for an economy. *AD*₁ and *SRAS*₁ represent the initial positions of the curves. *AD*₂ and *SRAS*₂ represent shifts in the positions of the curves.

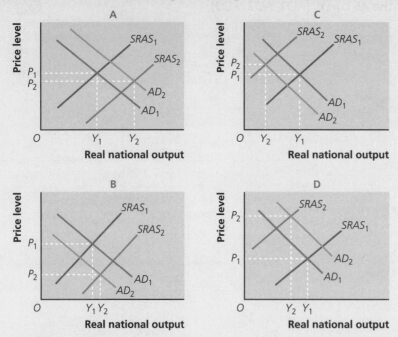

Which one of the diagrams, A, B, C or D, indicates the effect on the economy of a fall in wage rates and a fall in interest rates?

Exam-style questions: data response

40

20 Read Extracts A and B and answer the following questions.

Extract A

Consumers in 2014 were spending more on discretionary items such as cars, sport and going out. Transport became the biggest single item of expenditure in UK households — largely because nearly 2.5 million cars were sold in the UK in 2014. With inflation in 2015 close to zero for the whole year, households experienced strong rises in real incomes for the first time for a prolonged period — since before the 2008 crisis.

Some economists were worried that too much of this extra household spending was spent by borrowing money and that the higher consumption might lead to a re-run of the debt crisis that led to the last financial crash.

With oil prices falling throughout 2015 and other commodity prices also in decline, there seemed to be no sign of any significant upturn in inflation during 2016. This meant that interest rates were likely to remain lower than they otherwise would have been.

Extract B

Estimating the size of the multiplier is not as straightforward as it might seem in economic textbooks.

The size of the multiplier is clearly determined by how much spare capacity there is. For example, an economy operating at, or close to, capacity will see a multiplier of almost zero. In a deep recession, the multiplier may grow significantly large in size.

The type of extra spending in the economy may also affect the size of the multiplier. An increase in government expenditure is likely to have a greater effect than a cut in taxes — which may just be saved by consumers. Who is affected by the extra spending will also matter, as those with below average incomes are likely to spend a higher proportion of any additional income.

In the USA, it is estimated that the multiplier on increased government spending is 1.6. On tax cuts, however, the size of the multiplier falls to 1.

a **Other than changes in prices, state two factors which might lead to a rise in consumer spending.**

b **If there was an increase in government expenditure in the USA which led to a rise in GDP in that country of $8 billion, calculate the size of the original increase in government expenditure.**

c **Illustrate, using an *AD/AS* diagram, the effect of low oil prices and falling commodity prices.**

d Using an *AD/AS* diagram and the extracts, analyse the effects of higher interest rates on the performance of the UK economy.

16 marks

....

....

....

....

....

....

....

....

....

....

....

....

....

....

....

....

....

....

....

....

....

....

....

Exam-style questions: essay

60

Write your answers to the following questions on separate paper and attach them to your book.

21 a Analyse the main determinants of consumption in the UK economy. 15 marks

   b Evaluate the extent to which a government can decide what level of GDP it wishes the UK economy to produce. 25 marks

Topic 3

Economic performance

Economic growth and the economic cycle

In the long run, the economy's growth will be limited by the growth over time in the productive potential of the economy. However, in the short run, the variation of short-run growth from the long-term rate of growth — otherwise known as the trend growth — gives us the economic cycle.

Each stage of the economic cycle will generate different results for each indicator of the government's economic objectives. The deviation of short-run growth from long-run trend growth gives us output gaps (both positive and negative) in the economy. A number of explanations are provided to account for the economic cycle, such as excessive borrowing, speculation, animal spirits and herding.

Economic shocks will also occur which could have a supply-side or a demand-side cause. These can have significant unexpected positive or negative consequences for the macroeconomy.

1 Define the term 'output gap'. (AO1, AO2)   **3 marks**

2 Identify three explanations which may account for the economic cycle. (AO1)   **3 marks**

3 Explain how the multiplier–accelerator model can be used to explain the economic cycle. (AO1, AO2)   **5 marks**

4 The banking crisis of 2008 led to banks becoming unwilling to lend in a move to protect their own financial positions. Collapses in consumer confidence meant that households were unwilling to borrow money to spend, despite the cost of borrowing being at its lowest level ever.

Using an *AD/AS* diagram, analyse the impact of this economic shock, stating whether you believe this to be a demand-side or a supply-side shock. (AO1, AO2, AO3) `15 marks`

....

....

....

....

....

....

....

....

....

....

....

....

....

....

Employment and unemployment

Minimising unemployment is a key objective of the government. However, to minimise unemployment it is important to understand that there are various causes of unemployment in an economy; these include cyclical, frictional and structural causes. These types of unemployment can also be categorised as those caused by demand-side factors and those caused by supply-side factors. Unemployment can also be examined in terms of the concepts of voluntary and involuntary unemployment as well as the factors which determine real-wage unemployment. In addition, there is the natural rate of unemployment to consider.

There are consequences of unemployment both for individuals and for economic performance, which help one to understand the government's desire to reduce unemployment.

5 Distinguish between voluntary and involuntary unemployment. (AO1, AO2) `4 marks`

....

....

....

....

6 Using a diagram, show how an increase in the national minimum wage may lead to a higher level of unemployment. (AO1, AO2)   `4 marks`

7 Analyse the consequences of a high level of unemployment for the UK economy. (AO1, AO2, AO3)   `9 marks`

8 Analyse the factors which determine the natural rate of unemployment and explain why the term 'natural rate' may be misleading. (AO1, AO2, AO3)   `9 marks`

Inflation and deflation

Achieving stable prices is another key economic objective. Although low inflation is seen as desirable, governments will also wish to avoid deflation. Both inflation and deflation have consequences for individuals and the economy as a whole.

If a government is to manage inflation at a level it desires, it is important to understand what causes inflation. Inflation has two main causes: demand-pull and cost-push. Inflation can also be analysed using the monetarist model of the quantity theory of money.

It is also important to understand that commodity price changes as well as changes in the global external environment can have a significant effect on the inflation rate.

9 **Distinguish between disinflation and deflation. (AO1, AO2)** 4 marks

10 **Explain two negative consequences of inflation. (AO1, AO2)** 4 marks

11 **Using an *AD/AS* diagram, illustrate the concept of cost-push inflation, and show the impact on output and inflation of higher interest rates being used to reduce this type of inflation. (AO1, AO2)** 6 marks

12 **Analyse the reasons why a government wishes to keep inflation at a low and stable level. (AO1, AO2, AO3)** 9 marks

Macroeconomic policy conflicts

Output gaps are often characterised as leading to either unemployment or inflation, which may appear as a trade-off in attempting to achieve multiple objectives. This trade-off can also be represented by the short-run Phillips curve. The long-run Phillips curve is also considered, which attempts to address the fact that policy conflicts existing in the short run may not always exist in the long run.

13 Explain how the concept of opportunity cost can be used to explain a policy conflict. (AO1, AO2)

`4 marks`

14 Using a diagram, explain why the trade-off shown on the short-run Phillips curve may not exist in the long run. (AO1, AO2, AO3)

`10 marks`

15 'In the long run, the economy will always return to its natural rate of unemployment, which means there is no point attempting to reduce unemployment.' Explain the reasoning behind this statement and why it may be based on mistaken understanding. (AO1, AO2, AO3)

`9 marks`

Exam-style questions: multiple choice

Circle the letter of the answer that you think is correct.

16 The short-run Phillips curve illustrates a relationship between: `1 mark`

A The price level and the level of unemployment

B The rate of economic growth and the rate of inflation

C The rate of inflation and the rate of unemployment

D The wage rate growth and the rate of employment

17 The following chart shows actual and trend economic growth.

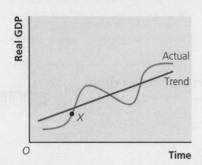

At point *X*, which of the following combinations of unemployment and inflation is most likely to occur? `1 mark`

	Inflation	Unemployment
A	Above average	Above average
B	Above average	Below average
C	Below average	Above average
D	Below average	Below average

18 Based on the quantity theory of money, which of the following would be most likely to lead to higher prices? `1 mark`

A Rising velocity of circulation, whilst output and money supply remain constant

B Rising money supply, whilst velocity of circulation falls and output remains constant

C Rising output and money supply, whilst velocity of circulation falls

D Rising money supply, whilst output increases and velocity of circulation falls significantly

Exam-style questions: data response

50

19 **Study Extracts A, B and C, and answer the following questions.**

Extract A

UK unemployment and CPI inflation, 2000–15

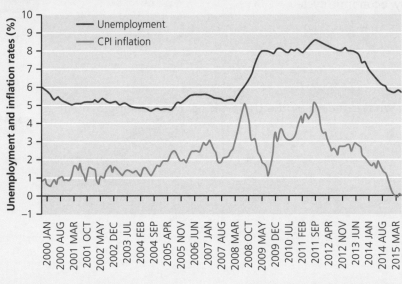

Source: www.economicshelp.org

Extract B

The idea of a 'textbook' economic cycle seems to be a concept which no longer applies since the 2008 financial crash. Sure, the recession was deep and inflation did fall. However, since the recovery started, the economy has not behaved as it should have done, according to standard economic textbooks.

Unemployment has fallen far quicker and by a far greater amount than anyone — including some at the Bank of England — actually expected. Given that growth in GDP was weak between 2009 and 2012, no one expected unemployment to go anywhere other than upwards, yet by 2015 it was back to where it was before the crash — with indications that it had further to fall.

Despite unemployment falling back to pre-crash levels, there has been no upward surge in inflation. If anything, prices have been reluctant to rise and inflation throughout 2015 remained close to zero for the full year.

Extract C

The traditional trade-off between unemployment and inflation seems to have disappeared for good. The Phillips curve used to illustrate the standard trade cycle concept that the economy could either grow quickly and unemployment fall, or grow slowly and inflation fall. However, some have argued that the trade-off no longer exists. This would be good news for the chancellor of the exchequer in 2015, who is looking for a fresh round of spending cuts in government expenditure without wanting to damage the high growth and low unemployment economy that the UK is becoming.

a In September 2011, the number of people who were unemployed was 2,503,000 according to the ILO. Using Extract A, calculate the approximate size of the UK labour force. **2 marks**

....

....

b Explain what is meant by 'economic cycle'. **4 marks**

....

....

....

....

c Using a diagram, explain what is meant by the trade-off between unemployment and inflation. **9 marks**

....

....

....

....

....

....

....

....

....

d To what extent can the government reduce unemployment in the long run? **25 marks**

Plan your answer below, then write it on separate paper and attach it to your book.

....

....

....

....

....

....

....

....

....

....

....

....

Exam-style questions: essay

60

20 **a** Analyse the main causes of inflation.

15 marks

b 'Governments should treat inflation and deflation exactly the same and take steps to avoid both.' Do you agree with this statement? Justify your answer.

25 marks

Plan your answer below, then write it on separate paper and attach it to your book.

Topic 4

Financial markets and monetary policy

The structure of financial markets and financial assets

The characteristics and functions of money are considered in this section, along with measures and definitions of the money supply — including narrow money and broad money. The differences between the money market, the capital market and the foreign exchange market are studied, as well as the role of the financial markets in the wider economy. Bond prices are examined as well as the differences between debt and equity.

1 State the four functions of money. (AO1) `4 marks`

2 Distinguish between narrow money and broad money. (AO1, AO2) `4 marks`

3 Distinguish between debt and equity. (AO1, AO2) `4 marks`

4 Explain the role of the forward market in terms of the foreign exchange market. (AO1, AO2) `3 marks`

5 Explain why there is an inverse relationship between bond prices and interest rates. (AO1, AO2)   `3 marks`

....

....

....

6 The initial bond price was £100 and the coupon on this bond was £1.25. The current yield on other bonds on the market is 1.5%. What price would you expect this bond to move towards? Explain your answer. (AO1, AO2)   `4 marks`

....

....

....

....

Commercial banks and investment banks

We can examine how banks create credit as well as the differences between commercial and investment banks. The objectives of commercial banks are concerned with liquidity, profitability and security, and these different objectives conflict with each other.

7 Briefly explain how a bank can create credit. (AO1, AO2)   `4 marks`

....

....

....

....

8 Distinguish between a commercial bank and an investment bank. (AO1, AO2)   `4 marks`

....

....

....

....

9 Explain the conflict between profitability and liquidity facing commercial banks. (AO1, AO2)   `4 marks`

....

....

....

....

Central banks and monetary policy

Here we focus on the main functions of a central bank. Monetary policy refers to changes in the price of money (the interest rate), the money supply and the availability of credit. Changes in monetary policy will affect the macroeconomic indicators. Interest rates are used mainly in the UK to manage the level of inflation and also economic growth as a secondary objective.

Changes in interest rates are decided monthly by the Monetary Policy Committee (MPC) of the Bank of England. These changes will not only affect growth, employment and inflation, but will also affect the exchange rate, which will indirectly affect other parts of the economy. We will consider how the Bank of England can influence the growth of the money supply.

10 Define the term 'quantitative easing'. (AO1)   `3 marks`

....

....

....

11 Briefly explain how the Bank of England achieves its remit of price stability in the UK. (AO1, AO2)   `4 marks`

....

....

....

....

12 Explain two ways in which a central bank can increase the supply of money in the economy. (AO1, AO2)   `6 marks`

....

....

....

....

....

....

Regulation of the financial system

The financial crisis of 2008 highlighted the potential for moral hazard within the banking system. In the aftermath of the crisis, the issue arose as to how to increase the degree of regulation of the banking industry without damaging the contribution made by this sector to the economy.

13 In the context of the banking system, explain the term 'moral hazard'. (AO1, AO2)   `4 marks`

....

....

14 Analyse two potential causes of a financial crisis. (AO1, AO2, AO3) **9 marks**

....

....

....

....

....

....

....

....

....

....

....

....

....

Exam-style questions: multiple choice

Circle the letter of the answer that you think is correct.

15 A bond is issued with a nominal value of £100 and the annual coupon is £2. When the bond was issued, it offered a return that was similar to other comparable securities. Three years later, the market rate of interest has fallen to 0.5%. This bond will not mature for many years yet. Calculate the approximate market price of this bond. **1 mark**

A £50   C £200

B £400   D £80

16 Which of the following types of bank is responsible for controlling the money supply in an economy? **1 mark**

A Commercial bank   C Central bank

B Investment bank   D Wholesale bank

17 Which of the following does the Bank of England's 'lender of the last resort' function not cover? **1 mark**

A Provision of liquidity to failing non-financial businesses during a recession

B Provision of liquidity to a bank with cash-flow difficulties

C Provision of liquidity to financial markets during a crisis

D Provision of liquidity to the banking system to meet the shortfalls in the banking system

18 Assets of a commercial bank would not include which of the following? **1 mark**

A Cash   C Government debt held

B Balances at the Bank of England   D Reserves (e.g. retained profits)

Exam-style questions: data response

19 Read Extracts A, B and C, and answer the following questions.

Extract A

The Funding for Lending Scheme (FLS) was introduced by the Bank of England and the Treasury (in 2012). Its aim is to increase the amount of lending made by commercial banks in the UK. It works by the Bank of England letting commercial banks borrow money from it more cheaply. This money can then be lent to businesses at a cheaper rate than they would otherwise have to pay.

Critics of the scheme point out that it has not actually led to any significant increase in lending by commercial banks and also has meant that the commercial banks do not have to try as hard as they would have done previously to attract savers; they now have an alternative source of money available.

Extract B

The growing buy-to-let property market in the UK could threaten financial stability and compound any boom and bust in house prices, according to the the Bank of England's Financial Policy Committee (FPC).

The 40% increase in the quantity of buy-to-let mortgage lending between 2008 and 2015 compares with an increase of just 2% in 'normal' owner-occupier mortgage lending. The share of buy-to-let in the number of outstanding mortgages has risen to 16% in 2015 from 12% in 2008.

The Bank said that buy-to-let landlords were much more likely to sell if there was a significant drop in house prices, causing property values to fall further, and a similar amplified effect could occur should prices go up sharply. The FPC was concerned that this might force buyers of property to take out even larger loans, thus increasing the risk to financial stability.

Extract C

Data on mortgages in the UK showed a rise in the demand for borrowing to buy houses. The number of UK mortgage approvals rose by 20% to 44,960 in November 2015 compared with a year earlier, whilst at the same time overall mortgage lending reached £12.8 billion in November, up 28% on the year.

a Using Extract C, calculate the number of UK mortgage approvals in November 2014. `2 marks`

....

....

....

b Explain why the Funding for Lending Scheme may not have been good for savers. `4 marks`

....

....

....

....

....

....

....

c Analyse the impact of increasing buy-to-let property on the performance of the UK economy.

9 marks

....

....

....

....

....

....

d To what extent is tighter bank regulation a good thing for UK economic performance?

25 marks

....

....

....

....

....

....

....

....

....

....

....

....

....

....

....

....

....

....

Exam-style questions: essay

20 **a** Analyse the factors which may have contributed to the 2008 financial crisis. `15 marks`

b 'Steps taken by the UK government should ensure that there is no repeat of the 2008 crisis.' Do you agree with this? Justify your view. `25 marks`

Plan your answer below, then write it on separate paper and attach it to your book.

Topic 5

Fiscal policy and supply-side policies

Fiscal policy

Changes in fiscal policy will affect both aggregate demand and aggregate supply. Fiscal policy and the resulting budget deficit or surplus will also have effects on the various macroeconomic indicators that the government is attempting to influence in achieving its objectives, as well as also having microeconomic effects.

The types of, and reasons, for both public expenditure and taxes will be considered. Taxes can be levied in the economy in a number of different ways, such as direct and indirect taxes.

1 Distinguish between an indirect tax and a direct tax. (AO1)　　**4 marks**

....

....

....

....

....

....

2 Distinguish between different types of government expenditure. (AO1, AO2)　　**4 marks**

....

....

....

....

....

....

3 Explain three reasons for government spending. (AO1, AO2)　　**6 marks**

....

....

....

....

....

....

....

....

4 Using a diagram, analyse the reasons why a government levies taxes on its population. (AO1, AO2, AO3)

15 marks

....

....

....

....

....

....

....

....

....

....

....

....

Supply-side policies

Long-run growth comes from increases in the productive capacity of the economy. This is referred to as the supply side of the economy. Improvements to this supply side can come from general supply-side improvements or specific supply-side policies.

Supply-side policies are often categorised into free-market supply-side policies, such as tax reform, privatisation, deregulation and some labour market reforms, or interventionist supply-side policies, such as spending on education and training, industrial policy and subsidies to encourage research and development. Supply-side policies can have both macroeconomic and microeconomic effects.

5 Give one example of a supply-side policy and one example of a supply-side improvement. (AO1)

2 marks

....

....

6 Explain how a tax cut can be both a microeconomic and a macroeconomic policy at the same time. (AO1, AO2)

4 marks

....

....

....

....

7 Analyse how improved 'labour market flexibility' will help to increase the long-run growth rate of the UK. (AO1, AO2, AO3)   `9 marks`

....

....

....

....

....

....

....

....

....

....

....

....

....

Exam-style questions: multiple choice

Circle the letter of the answer that you think is correct.

8 Which of the following is true about the national debt?   `1 mark`

  A The debt will grow each year the government runs a trade deficit

  B The national debt will rise if there is a budget surplus

  C The national debt as a percentage of GDP will always rise if there is any budget deficit

  D The national debt will rise if there is a budget deficit

9 A tax which accounts for a greater proportion of the incomes of those from low-income households is most likely to be described as: `1 mark`

  A Progressive   C Direct

  B Regressive   D Proportional

10 Which of the following would be classed as a supply-side policy?   `1 mark`

  A Cuts in income tax designed to increase consumption

  B Cuts in interest rates designed to boost aggregate demand

  C Improved innovation in an economy due to a change in entrepreneurial attitudes

  D Reductions in government spending on welfare to affect work incentives

11 'The budget balance is in deficit only because economic growth has remained well below average for a number of years.' What economic concept does this statement describe?   `1 mark`

  A Cyclical budget deficit   C Cyclical budget surplus

  B Structural budget deficit   D National debt

Exam-style questions: data response

12 Read Extracts A, B and C, and answer the following questions.

Extract A

Given the persistent deficit on the government's finances in 2016, many have looked to new ways in which taxes can be used to raise revenue to finance public expenditure. Many of these types of tax have not been implemented in the UK, but they have certainly been considered by a government keen to close the deficit as soon as possible.

Several countries in eastern Europe have introduced a flat tax — a single fixed rate of tax paid by all, regardless of income. The benefit of a flat tax is that it does not penalise those on high incomes and therefore encourages people to earn more. However, some say the flat tax would be unfair.

A tax on financial activities has also been proposed. This would involve a small percentage levied as a tax on transactions involving currencies, bonds and shares. It is believed that such a tax — originally proposed by the Nobel Prize-winning economist, James Tobin — if imposed globally could raise billions. However, some have argued that this would only work if all countries agreed to participate in implementing the tax.

A mansion tax was proposed by some political parties in previous general elections in the UK. This would place a tax on those who had high-value properties (say, valued at over £2 million in the UK). However, some argued that the tax is impractical as it confuses a household's wealth with household income.

Extract B

In 2015 the first £10,600 of income earned was a tax-free allowance. Incomes in excess of this tax-free allowance were taxed as follows.

Income level	Tax rate
£10,600–£42,385	20%
£42,386–£150,000	40%
Over £150,000	45%

Extract C

George Osborne, the UK chancellor of the exchequer, is pushing forward a plan to make governments legally obliged to run a budget surplus in normal economic times. As long as growth in the economy is reasonably healthy, a government would have to collect more in tax than the total of public expenditure.

Some have welcomed this move as it will make a repeat of the record-breaking budget deficit experienced in the UK in recent years impossible. However, a counter-argument is that the proposed law makes no real distinction between types of government spending. This may mean that a government has to cut vital spending on infrastructure — crucial to boosting long-run economic growth — in order to achieve a budget surplus.

a **Using Extract B, calculate the amount of income tax paid on earnings of (i) £18,000; (ii) £48,000.** **2 marks**

....

....

....

....

....

b Explain one benefit of maintaining a progressive system of taxation for
   UK incomes.   `4 marks`

c Analyse the causes of long-run growth in the UK.   `9 marks`

d Using Extract C, to what extent is a law to make governments run budget
   surpluses likely beneficial for the UK economy?   `25 marks`

Exam-style questions: essay

13 **a** Analyse how taxes can affect economic activity. 15 marks

b To what extent should government spending be tightly controlled and not used to manage the economy? 25 marks

Plan your answer below, then write it on separate paper and attach it to your book.

Topic 6

The international economy

Globalisation

Globalisation is caused by many different factors. Multinational corporation (MNCs) have affected less developed countries in their objective of becoming developed. However, MNCs can also have negative effects on economies.

1 **Define the term 'globalisation'. (AO1)** `3 marks`

....
....
....

2 **Describe three factors that have led to increased globalisation. (AO1, AO2)** `6 marks`

....
....
....
....
....
....
....

3 **Analyse the benefits to a multinational corporation of being allowed access to operate in less developed countries. (AO1, AO2, AO3)** `9 marks`

....
....
....
....
....
....
....
....
....
....
....

41

Trade

The theory of international trade in terms of absolute and comparative advantage shows the benefits of specialisation and trade. However, there will still be costs incurred with international trade. The pattern of international trade between the UK and the rest of the world has changed over time.

Countries may adopt a range of protectionist policies, such as tariffs, quotas and export subsidies. Arguments are made both to justify the imposition of protectionist measures and to oppose them.

Customs unions, such as the EU, will affect a country's pattern of trade. The WTO seeks to promote free trade globally.

---

4 Define the term 'absolute advantage'. (AO1)　　　　`3 marks`

....

....

5 Define the term 'comparative advantage'. (AO1)　　　　`3 marks`

....

....

6 Briefly explain the role of the WTO. (AO1, AO2)　　　　`4 marks`

....

....

....

7 Explain two features of a customs union. (AO1, AO2)　　　　`4 marks`

....

....

....

....

8 Using a diagram, analyse how a tariff will help protect an economy from foreign trade. (AO1, AO2, AO3)　　　　`9 marks`

....

....

....

....

....

....

....

....

....

The balance of payments

The balance of payments consists of the current account, the capital account and the financial account. The current account itself is split into trade in goods, trade in services, primary income and secondary income.

Factors which affect the current account balance (such as a deficit or surplus) include productivity, inflation and the exchange rate. There are a number of policies — expenditure-switching and expenditure-reducing — that can be used to correct a current account deficit. These can have an impact on other macroeconomic policy objectives.

Deficits and surpluses on the current account for an economy can be significant, and so can investment flows between countries.

9 State three components of the balance of payments. (AO1)   3 marks

10 State three policies that could be used to correct a current account deficit. (AO1)   3 marks

11 Distinguish between foreign direct investment and portfolio investment. (AO1, AO2)   4 marks

12 From the following data, calculate the current account balance for the economy. (AO1, AO2)   4 marks

	£ million
Exports of goods	425,225
Imports of goods	640,411
Exports of services	31,231
Imports of services	29,808
Primary income balance	4,451
Secondary income balance	(1,132)

13 Explain briefly how expenditure-reducing policies would help to reduce a current account deficit. (AO1, AO2)   4 marks

Exchange rate systems

The exchange rate is determined by a number of factors such as foreign trade and interest rates. A government can choose to allow the exchange rate to float freely or can intervene either to manage its float or to fix the exchange rate. Systems of exchange rate management (fixed and floating) have both advantages and disadvantages. There is a further case to be assessed about whether to join a currency union such as the eurozone.

14 Define the term 'exchange rate'. (AO1) `3 marks`

....

....

15 If £1 = $1.67 and £1 = €1.33, calculate the price of $1 in euros (€). (AO1, AO2) `2 marks`

....

....

16 Income per capita in France is €48,000, and in the USA it is $62,000. If £1 = €1.35 and $1 = €0.95, calculate the income per capita in both countries expressed in pounds. (AO1, AO2) `4 marks`

....

....

....

....

17 State three determinants of a country's exchange rate. (AO1) `3 marks`

....

....

....

18 Analyse the impact on the economy of a government attempting to fix its exchange rate against another currency. (AO1, AO2, AO3) `9 marks`

....

....

....

....

....

....

....

....

....

....

....

Economic growth and development

Economic growth and development are linked but are distinct economic concepts. Less developed economies have common characteristics and there are some indicators that help us to distinguish between the levels of development within an economy, such as the Human Development Index (HDI).

There are factors that will help both economic growth and development (such as investment, education and training), but also factors that act as barriers to growth and development (such as corruption, institutional barriers, poor infrastructure, inadequate human capital and a lack of property rights).

Certain economic policies will help an economy to grow and to develop, and aid and trade will help in promoting both of these aspects.

19 State three indicators that combine to form the Human Development Index (HDI). (AO1)   3 marks

20 Explain the difference between economic growth and economic development. (AO1, AO2)   4 marks

21 Explain three factors which contribute to preventing an economy from reaching developed status. (AO1, AO2)   6 marks

22 Analyse the policies that a less developed country can implement to move closer to reaching development. (AO1, AO2, AO3)   9 marks

Exam-style questions: multiple choice

Circle the letter of the answer that you think is correct.

23 The table below shows the data relating to an economy's current account over a 2-year period, expressed in £ billions.

	Balance of trade in goods	Balance of trade in services	Primary income balance	Secondary income balance
Year 1	200	−180	40	−15
Year 2	220	−150	20	−35

Which of the following can be concluded from the above data?

A   The current account deficit worsened

B   The balance of payments was in surplus

C   The current account balance in year 1 was £60 billion in surplus

D   The current account balance in year 2 had improved by £10 billion

24 In the UK, the value of the exchange rate changes over time from £1 = €1.10 to £1 = €1.40. Which of the following is likely to occur as a result of the change in the exchange rate?

A   UK imports from the countries using the euro will become more expensive

B   UK exports will increase due to improved price competitiveness

C   The current account of the balance of payments is likely to worsen in the long term

D   The current account of the balance of payments is likely to improve after worsening initially

25 A country decides to use foreign protection to eliminate a current account deficit. Which of the following would not be an appropriate argument to justify this protection? **1 mark**

A   Protection will lead to improved choice and lower prices for consumers

B   Developing industries can be allowed to grow without the threat of cheaper foreign competition

C   Jobs can be protected in the local economy as a result

D   Foreign competition which benefits from unfair subsidies can be limited by protection

26 Which of the following would not count as an inflow on the UK's balance of payments? **1 mark**

A   Dividends paid to a UK owner on profits earned by a company located in France

B   Wages sent back to the UK families of workers located within Germany

C   UK firms opening new enterprises in Italy

D   Imports of goods by Spanish residents from a UK car manufacturer

Exam-style questions: data response

60

27 **Study Extracts A, B and C, and answer the following questions.**

Extract A

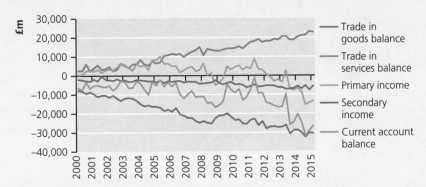

UK current account, 2000–15

Extract B

In 2014, the current account deficit reached 5.5% of GDP, which was the largest deficit since records began in 1948. However, there are many who claim that the large deficit does not matter. It is pointed out that the balance of payments must always balance and so a deficit on the current account must be matched by a surplus elsewhere in the balance of payments, i.e. the financial account and the capital account.

The large current account deficit is attributed not just to declining performance on net exports but also to the gradual deterioration of the primary income balance, which has moved further into deficit.

As long as the UK can finance the current account deficit, it is claimed that the current account balance does not matter. It will only matter when investors decide not to lend to the UK, and whilst there is great uncertainty across the eurozone, and whilst UK economic growth outpaces that of most other countries, this is unlikely to happen.

Extract C

As the current account deficit has approached 6% of GDP, some economists have grown increasingly concerned. Although they feel the prevailing opinion is that the current account deficit no longer matters in a world of floating exchange rates, they have raised several points which suggest that it might still matter.

Some have warned that if the deficit grows in size or remains in deficit for a prolonged period, investors will begin to become nervous and will be less willing to fund the current account deficit by placing money into the UK. This may force interest rates higher. There is also the fear that, as investors withdraw money, the exchange rate will fall rapidly, precipitating a sterling crisis.

a **Define the term 'current account deficit'.**   `3 marks`

....

....

b **Explain why 'the balance of payments must always balance'.**   `3 marks`

....

....

c **Analyse policies that could be used to reduce or eliminate the current account deficit.**

`9 marks`

....
....
....
....
....
....
....
....
....

d **Using the information found in the extracts, evaluate to what extent it matters that the UK has a large current account deficit**

`25 marks`

Write your answer on a separate sheet.

Exam-style questions: essay

`60`

Write your answers to the following questions on separate paper and attach them to your book.

28 a **Analyse the characteristics of a less developed economy.**

`15 marks`

b **Is foreign aid useful in helping countries achieve development? Justify your answer.**

`25 marks`

Hodder Education, an Hachette UK company, Blenheim Court, George Street, Banbury, Oxfordshire OX16 5BH

Orders
Bookpoint Ltd, 130 Park Drive, Milton Park, Abingdon, Oxfordshire OX14 4SB
tel: 01235 827827
fax: 01235 400401
e-mail: education@bookpoint.co.uk
Lines are open 9.00 a.m.–5.00 p.m., Monday to Saturday, with a 24-hour message answering service.
You can also order through the Hodder Education website:
www.hoddereducation.co.uk

© David Horner and Steve Stoddard 2016
ISBN 978-1-4718-4462-1

First printed 2016
Impression number 5 4 3 2 1
Year 2020 2019 2018 2017 2016

This guide has been written specifically to support students preparing for the AQA A-level Economics examinations. The content has been neither approved nor endorsed by AQA and remains the sole responsibility of the authors.

Typeset by Aptara

Printed in Spain

Hachette UK's policy is to use papers that are natural, renewable and recyclable products and made from wood grown in sustainable forests. The logging and manufacturing processes are expected to conform to the environmental regulations of the country of origin.

ISBN 978-1-4718-4462-1